MOTION in POETRY

MOTION in POETRY

WOMEN'S PRESS | TORONTO

MOTION in POETRY
by Motion (Wendy Brathwaite)

The first paperback edition published in 2002 by
Women's Press
180 Bloor Street West, Suite 1202
Toronto, Ontario
M5S 2V6

www.womenspress.ca

Women's Press acknowledges the financial support of the Government of Canada through the Book Publishing Industry Development Programme for our publishing activities.

NATIONAL LIBRARY OF CANADA CATALOGUING IN PUBLICATION DATA

Motion, 1970-
    Motion in poetry / Motion (Wendy Brathwaite).
ISBN 0-88961-401-6

    1. Title.

PS8576.O77M68 2002   C811'.6   C2002-901769-6
PR9199.4.M68M68 2002

COVER & BOOK DESIGN Zab Design & Typography
COVER PHOTOGRAPHY Chanel Kennebrew
Log On! www.motionlive.com

02 03 04 05 06 07 08   6 5 4 3 2 1

Printed and bound in Canada by Transcontinental Printing

Foreword

In '82 and '83, new Dub poet groove
Come howlin', growlin', and bustin' moves,
Outta Domestic Bliss, a Carib-Can crew—
Lillian Allen, Devon Haughton, Clifton Joseph too—
Shakin' T.O. wid some goddamn trut's,
Bout Rhythm an' Hard Times, Roots
And Culture, and Metropolitan Blues:
Immigration discrimination, cops' shots loose,
Too many dead boys and Black folks pinched,
In Regent Park, Oakwood-Vaughan, Jane and Finch.
So Allen, Haughton, and Joseph shout out rage,
Callin' fire down on "Babylon" from the stage,
With smooth Marley rhythm and Last Poets' raps,
Incisive Sistren vision and Kwesi Johnson naps.
They set example, some reggae you sample:
See, they dream phat and their diction's real ample.
And check out Dionne Brand, this sistuh also comes
Straight outta orature and tall Gayap drums,
With cantos and songs espousin' liberation,
Exposin' downpression sans any hesitation,
And prayin' for revolt and praisin' Mandela,
Soundin' sumpin' like Ahdri Zhina Mandiela,

Who also wrings music out the written word,
Performin' it, stormin' it, as you must've heard.
Folks, the scene's big, but it gotta make room,
For Wendy Brathwaite, Motion, her sonic poems:
She got the class, she got the sass,
She rock the mic like an earthquake in the grass.
Us old-school poets set the stage, uh huh,
And Motion, she study our page, uh huh,
Givin' props to her peeps and agitation to the age.
A Son of Solomon singer, an Ecclesiastes sage,
She preach "One love" and she teach unity—
To make bro's and sistuhs into one community.
If you got the notion,
To read imagination and emotion,
You need a potent poetry potion:
Ladies and gentlemen, give it up for Motion!

George Elliott Clarke
Department of English
University of Toronto
December mmi

Give Thanx

family of mine

friends of mine

teachers of mine

loves of mine

Spirit Divine

* * *

Livication

For those who came before

and those to come...

MOTION IN POETRY

Rap and spoken word are the oral culture of today, the stories of the times that we live in. Urban dwellers have built a culture from four elements: DJing, Breakdancing, Graffiti Art, and the modern day Griot — the MC.

An MC's words are most often heard on records, CDs and over mics, accompanied by beats and rhythms. Yet each script is born within the "rhymebook" that holds the lyrics and poetics of the rappers who speak the text. Today's Griot spit soul hitting words that resonate with musical punctuation.

Motion In Poetry grows from my life — my passion for music and words expressed on the page, the airwaves and the stage. *Motion In Poetry* bridges the worlds of the rhymed, spoken and written word. I want to represent for the cipher of MCs who can shine on paper, by bringing the movement of Hip Hop music and culture to my poetry.

Like the lyrics of Blues, beat poets of Jazz, and dub poetry of Reggae, Hip Hop and spoken word are the experience of a generation growing in states of "otherness" throughout the world, striving to create and affirm identity. *Motion In Poetry* is Toronto, the *Northside and beyond.*

Motion In Poetry is me... Word, Sound, Power.

Peace.

TABLE OF CONTENTS

15 In Motion...

16 What it is...

18 Girl

21 Strong

27 Black Woman Rage

30 Write a Culturally Specific Haiku with Internal Rhyme

32 Livicated to the Pisces

BOOM BAP

37 Rhyme On My Mind *Pt. 1*

39 Knowledge Wisdom & Overstanding

41 Soul Track

43 The Trilogy [3 MCz]

47 nine/won/one

49 Midnite

55 Tale of 2 Cities

57 Dangerous

62 Losing My Religion

65 The Lottery

67 Freestyle

70 Living It...

75 Street Signs

79 Street Vibes

81 I-Land

84 For Ja(h)son

88 Panther

90 Black & White

95 Revelation

97 No Title

98 Residential

105 Regrets

107 Hideaway

109 Free

112 The Lesson

114 Dear Marky

117 Life Sentence

119 Cycle of Life

123 For Kwesro (R.I.P.)

127 Negus

129 Rhyme Mind My Mind *Pt. 2*

131 This Is My 1st Time

133 Mmmmmm

136 Dear_____

138 The Door

141 Rollo

143 Invasion of the Booty Snatcha

152 Scene

153 Sweetness

160 March 11

162 Oh

166 J'ouvert

MOTION IN POETRY

in motion…

When I was young I used to wonder what I'd do with my life:
How many babies would I mother?
Would I be someone's wife?
My mental vision always seemed to be including a mic
I didn't know that I'd be married to these tunes that I write
See in this thing you're in it from your start to your finish
Inspired by higher powers and my
poetic visuals
Words become material
my life's the subject
Erupting so I can build my own republic
I was twelve when I designed my manifesto
Came in a dream
from that night, there's been no rest, *yo*
I confess:
I had to grow the heart of a lioness
Progress like a vet while I'm applying it
I didn't choose to MC
I got assigned
Been seeded with a gene that has me fiending to rhyme
Hopping trains, planes and buses to take me on my next trip
Next time… *the Mothership.*

WHaT IT IS…

for Zulu Nation

"Hip Hop is manifest of an oppressed reality" *
This is key
Creativity is the essence of our livity
Uniquely I'm proof of an abundance of substance
and what I see
is Hip Hop, God and me
Creating all together now
a music representin'
non-convention
Civilizations up to heaven
Given plenty of insight
Tho' sometimes my vision's blurry
But my third eye's expanding so the truth should never hurt me
Just makes me more thirsty for instant satisfaction
What can I do if shit is hidden
Just pretend it never happened?
Leave the devil laughing
Pursue in his institution
Pay for his illusions
so I can survive in this confusion?

Decisions, decisions
the White House or Wisdom
A poor woman's prison
or a Parliamentary position
Politics make me sick
No treats without tricks
Street disciples in the mix
of mayhem and madness
In this metropolis we're just a digit on chip
But the ghetto level's distinctly documented by the script that I design
Defining with a new state of mind
Motion's moving on *like time...*

Pee Wee Dance, Zulu Nation Anniversary, NYC, 1996.

GIRL
for Jennifer

I remember when we used to play
Black and white barbies at the old house
The bottom floor stored a dollhouse,
lots of clothes, and home-made
outfits.
We danced in the basement
held annual beauty pageants
sat on the roof and ate
cupcakes and fruits.
I held you as you climbed or
you held me, but
none of us ever fell.
We sat in the sun.
We dreamed of life,
made grand plans of
apartments, husbands and
boyfriends.
Chose children's names
and superstar
spouses,
We sold junk on the curb.

Made concoctions of
cream, water and grease
braided tightly knitted hair,
tried on eye shadow.
Talked about boys,
cried when the bleeding came.
I envied your style,
confidence
daring.
I prided in the title
"best friend."
I laughed loudly at jokes,
shared in private codes —
whispered *"the beans are in the can..."*
when parental ears
threatened to
capture our secrets like
big pitchers.

We grew, danced,
walked, late nites
sweated in basement
parties
wrote notes
complained
fought
rewound funny parts
in videos —
over and over

and over again.
Grabbed our sides
rolled on floors
gave high-fives,

Said good-bye.

STRONG

for the little sistas

What can I say today
when asked to bring
right words to
bright minds
living on the brink of fast times
accessing a world over phone lines
Striving in a world of *get mine*
I ask myself today
what can I say...

What can I say to
today's millennial female
growing knowing the intimate details of
downloading on dot.coms
spitting the words to latest rap songs
Given a mission to trod over worlds beyond
in sneaks with fat knapsacks,
fly hairstyles and
it's on...

But what can I say...
When I see little women driven
with the skills to build
succeed with success
given the intuition to survive the stress
Walking with *"heads high"*
like a fly goddess
Not content to possess the
title of "weaker sex"
Not settling for less
Not taking 2nd best
Not giving away what's most precious
No con-test...

But what can I say?
to souls who probably already knew...
that for a brief moment in time
I wished it was me
that was you
Sitting here with my girls back in
eighty-two
Being given the tools to do what
I had to do
Told that I too could be
Beautiful and fruitful and
Able to have all I ever wanted to
That everything that I ever believed about myself
would always come true —
That no one could distract me unless

I allowed them to
That I could
do for self
That I should
never fear to ask for help

That I was passion in the making and
deeper understanding
That I was born to be...

That I could wake up the world and say
A mi dis...
This is me
this is what my mother *tried* to show me I could be

But forget the coulda, shoulda, wouldas
Each day is a new reality
Gives me hope
Living's all the drama I need
Forget the soaps
Cause life's the mystery
and *"We ain't going nowhere..."*
We're making history —
"R.E.S.P.E.C.T."
Check the *"Soul Sista Soul Sista"*
Sheroes with old souls
and the power to bring life
to those who are
yet to be...

This is *her*story
Discovering the glory that
glows like a fire this time
Divinely designed
Wisdom
Woman-kind
What a precious thing to be
What a deep, *deep*
responsibility...

I know what I can say
to today's millennial females
growing knowing the
intimate details of
URLs, chat rooms and dot.coms
MP3s, videos,
DVDs and CD ROMs
Ladies born to know that they
got it going on...

That *you* are the continuation
of a vibe that's strong and
that *you* manifest a blessing
of a line that's long

That you can
Stay strong
Live strong
Think strong
Keep strong

That you can be
Gentle and strong
Humble and strong
Confident and strong
Human and strong

And despite all the tears that will come in your night
And despite those wrong moves that's gonna blurry your sight
Despite all these haters that make you wanna fight
Despite the times it's so hard to follow your first mind
and do what you *know* is right
When fools try to bite
and your pockets are tight
When you're running through the dark
and it feels like you'll never see the light

Girl...
"Everything's gonna be alright
Everything's gonna be alright
Everything's gonna be alright, now..."

Truss me...
Don't worry if on the journey sometimes it gets a little dusty
"Cause if 1st you don't succeed..."
Seen?

'Cause S is for Survival
T is for the Trials
R is for the Road that we travel over the miles

O's for Opportunities to
open doors that knocking
N's for natural beauty and you know that we be flaunting
G's got it going on
Girl, you got it going on
Giving all we got and getting back
so we keep building on top
It don't stop
Worth more than a million
Like the bright moon and
shining sun
So Girl,
Stay strong.

BLack woman RaGe

Black Woman rage makes us take to the stages
Up front at rallies
Leading black families
Black woman rage is a thing of beauty
Doing our duty,
making our roles
Suffering in silence, giving the bad eye
Calling on God,
dealing with spirits
Jah-Jah takes over as riddims move hips
Cusses come from full brown female lips
Black woman rage is a sight to behold
Working the fields
suns beat on bent backs
Black songs rise with density of deep sound
Deep pasts seep to all who have the ear —
Can you understand the meaning
of Rage… Black… Woman… Song?
Sad, true, throaty, tired
Awakened
As we stretch to the heights of creation

Leggo our hand in the offending face
Stay in our place? What place?
When we just be all over...
Never removed as we feed the masses
with milk, poems and minds
Full breasts and asses
Queen Nzinga looks on
as we swing our small axes
through the forests of fearsome shadows
that mean us no good
We learn to run from home-grown licks
Give 2 snaps up
and stand akimbo
as only Raging Black Women could.
We beat the drums to call on the sisters
to pass on the secrets that only mothers know.
two hundred and forty days of
two heart-beats, two sighs,
two souls, two-fold life-form multiply
with the powers of Yin and Yang
One moment kisses to heal the sting of her strong hand
Raging, Woman Black —
back to the basics of the Motherland...
Speak your story, speak
sister songs
and weep if you will
at the rage that kept us frozen, still
under humping weights
that pinned us in darkened places

Rage that kept us from killing our rapists
In order to maintain we paralyzed ourselves instead
They left us for dead
They *thought* we were
dead
But we don't die,
we...
grow, laugh, spread, cry
Daughters of the cotton and cane
cannot wither and die.

write a culturally specific haiku with internal rhyme

Me, I am a moth —
Er of pepper-pot dreams, see.
Melange in rap songs.

Check it. Wicked tracks.
Jack — na badda me, see, fe
Mi rhyme style is wile.

Bathurst first — then run
Pon Eglinton. Stand and stare.
Brown/Black faces there.

Yes. Coo-coo an' fish
Sweet an' nice — rice an' peas, please
Tease delightfully.

Don't front — you're open
I got them trapped in my rap —
Rhymes to be exact.

Nappy heads swing dreads
As The Roots move the youth to
Prove that we love life.

What's up Mr. White
You've been up all nite trying
To be just like me.

inspiredbytraciemorris&cliftonjoseph @ fresharts '95

LIVICATED TO THE PISCES

All the Pisces danced that day
The first of '95
for we all knew
the Pisces age had
Just come alive.
We live in knowing strengths beyond
The doors that others see.
The Pisces danced, and skanked
and moved
To Tribe, Rakim, Marley.
They praised with bodies —
Spun and stomped —
in ecstasy and pride.
The Pisces danced, and chant and
sang
A Sagittarius by their side
To keep them steady as the rock moved on.
With minds in clouds and suns
the Pisces *rised*, with wings to fly
And chant this Babylon down.

brooklynnewyork

BOOm BaP

RHYME ON MY MIND *Pt. I*

When I was younger
I used to wonder
how I would handle
The life that I was given — living like I'm on a trampoline
Feelin' the seconds jump from days to months
To years, some of my peers now be lying in dust
Ashes to ash — used to skip class
but now I teach it
Reaching my goals
Tho I was told I couldn't reach it
Music is pursuit for fools
and maybe dreamers getting caught in the floss
Getting lost and always scheming for that next deal
Impossible to put the pen to the side
— picking formats of logic —
I never meant to be ostracized
but to realize my vision
Come in the night like a lady in white
bringing the insight
So I write because have to
Release the locks that got my brain all blocked

and backed up
I'm acting up when I'm repressing
Tryna progress
and clear my ears so I can finally hear the lesson.

KNOWLEDGE WISDOM & OVERSTANDING

Give me the mic so I can slay all these amateurs
Kill they bull and slash 'em up like a matador
Tongue is my sword, you're left extinct like a dinosaur
I resurrect, and never die
like I was here before
The second I was given the pen
Opened my tongue
Let the powers of the ancestors run
Harder they come
They gotta fall for even thinking of out-thinking my style
Not equipped to read the script that's codified in my file
They found our scriptures on Egyptian walls
Locked in the Vatican
and vaults under the Taj Mahal
Feminine wile
Women with medicine
Battlescars like veterans
Fools say I'm unsettling
Their careers, we're wrecking them
Downsize 'em
Neutralize 'em

They demise in they depravity
Hip Hop has got a hole
and I was born to fill the cavity
With the last word with Black Pearl
to bounce up in your stereo
We heavier than hard dough
and you're hollow like a cheerio
Nah badda test the goddess that holds the key to your destiny
Motion say that vengeance is mine, and you're vexing me

Realize that melanin will breed intelligent women
So take you lies and fiction
We don't need none a dem

SOUL TRACK

We in a war but don't know it
Smoke weed but don't grow it
Take heed, but don't show it
Your mind and body I blow it
Rock boats and row 'em
Wherever you got your notion
To try test Mo
You're lost in your high tech gloss
The rawest rhymes galorist
Best prearrange with your florist
Cause at the end the night you're hist'
Not a story
My brain's been a rap laboratory
from the one-two
Mic check
It's coming tru'
Ya dun know some plunder
Others will pillage my global village
But never mind we never die, still
They can't overstand the fam that ran
the original land

Made man from sand
Hold the whole world in her hand
Some backhand but I plan grand schemes
No scams, no blasphemes
blowing off steam
900 degrees
and your deep freeze is shattered
Muthafuckas I battered
they only scattered
Like the shaft the wind driveth away
This first Psalm
disperse harm out my way
So *salaam*
Follow I
Maintain calm as I
set the bomb
3 bills and 60 seconds and it's on
I embalm you like an Egyptian
My inscription exhumes all your fiction
The *raw deal* is real
Give 'em something they can feel
The rhymes I wield
Clearing your whole battle-field.

THE TRILOGY [3 MCz]

featuring Apani B. Fly and Tara Chase

Apani B. Fly:

    NYC, FLO to Q Boro to T.Dot

    Bang heavy on beats

    Apani meets Motion means action

    Women we make it happen

    Bring it like Bruce kicks ass in flicks

    Legit lip service

    Politic but fuck Nervous

    and Wreck business

    Peep files from the ambitious

    Sounds vicious

    The way I word this is perfect

    Sick and cancerous

    I dust you up

    Flip a tuff routine

    Blow posers to smithereens

    They wonder how I mean

    I guess I'm just too damn potent

    Eliminate and slay niggas like a cop making quotas

    Hold up!

    I feel the call of the base

I'm slave to the rhythm
Native to the ways of the streets
Give my love to Queens for molding me
Hip Hop for showing me
Fans for quoting me
Friends for knowing me
You know it's on again
Bout to kill a mic tonight then I'm gone again
Then it's home to record another song again
I gotta have it so I'm killing top billing

Motion:
Turn up your dial to the triple "O"
Ozone layers I blow
Blasting holes in you cosmos
Orally flowin over your town, *yo*
Get the connects
Extra correct
Mental and physical fit
Check the aspect
Naturally inclined, Apani be flying
Air Can to the north land with a mic in her hand
Mo lighting up you spine like a live wire
Blowing outta control like bond fires
We blazing!
Come fe bun down your station
The war is on
Nah badda test the Amazon
You got questions?

Here's the subject:
How to drop a bomb and erupt shit
We live and direct
Who woulda knew that this notorious two
wid a crew up in the studio would stew you up a brew
It's potent
My last shit was quoted
Couldn't underestimate the lick when I wrote it
Got a load on my chest
Dropping joints with all the points I stress
Got inspired by a higher highness to drop
Check the Q-spot
to the T.Dot
giving all we got
Whut...

Tara Chase:

Came in on the unexpected
Undetected
Move like smooth like
Crew when connected
Download
Hitting your brain
Hitting your veins
Hitting your thoughts
Making the process insane
Maintain
Over the rhythm I'm spitting in 'em
Making it known I'm too large

Never fittin' in 'em
Swimmin' in 'em
like me in a size thirty
Runnin outta breath on tracks
I'm too wordy
Blaziatic!
Still quick with grammatics
Flip it though I'm tired as hell and asthmatic
Got you on the wall ready to fall
Like first time cutting the ice ever at all
Look to your left
Now to the right
We got the sick combination
plus mad insight
Taking flight
would be your best decision
Since skill level will only force you to submission.

nɪne/won/one

I'm looking out my
window @ cool blocks
vibrations @ bus stops
bus rocks my rhythm to rhyme offa my skull top
A second to reckon my past
It couldn't last
got caught up in the flash
but failed to stash my cash
Thought life was like *forever*
All tears, some laughs
Wished that I could grow up
but still be 20 and a half
Now my eyes watch scenarios
that's realer than blood-baths
over oceans, the scuds crash
right here trades mash
humans into metal and glass
wipe the smile off my mask
they taking terror to task — making cage for dat ass
mad sad days while we waving the flag
digging through trash — graves by the mass

I pass
I hadda wake up
but still like walking a dream
and talking a dream
Hoping like King to put some hope in this thing
Feeling shaky like I'm walking a string
tight squeeze up in the middle of the dope and its fiend

Just a little bit longer
waiting 'til I'm a little bit stronger
or richer or bigger till I deliver with full force
The full course got served up
Before we know dessert's up
too late to get worked up
Chains become digital
Control, subliminal
Independence is criminal
Kids are getting cynical
times are real
wanna cling to my umbilical
Write lines with swiftness
while time is minimal
I watch the cool blocks
vibrations @ bus stops
bus rocks my rhythm
I write off my skull top
Snatch a second to consider my past
It couldn't last
got caught up in the flash
I shoulda stashed some cash.

MIDNITE

It's about midnite. My pockets are tight
but still I'm rushing to look real right
joining the line in which I'm shoving
with other bodies. Getting uptight to feel the blue
lights shine upon my skin
on the dim dance floor.

I want more, *most* of the time — but sometimes
a loud distraction's all I have —
A little bit of sinful interaction as the
boom beats the ear — my red makes it greater.
One jam gets me open
till the master with the fader got me —

Filled to the hilt with instant satisfaction.
Eyes scoping —
Watchin' bad man with they backs dem
Glued up to the wall.
B-boys in the middle fall.
The hole opens up like a chasm.
Backs spasm.

The next joint's a higher happening, escalating.
By the door, more ladies come wading in.
Now the trickle is a sea of ancient faces,
and ancient traces up in the scene
as mean riddims lick my vision.

Half closed eyes reveal prisms of dark lights,
steam rising from lips holding the spark.
Strobes deflect from a bottle raised
to set the dark on fire.
Just for a second, it's too good.
I'll think of heaven in the morrow.
For now, my sorrows get drowned
by speaker sounds.

But damn:
Suddenly I get awoken
My high daze becomes a haze of bodies.
Above the music, girl screams erupt the party.
Stampeding feet fall heavy —
laying the beat with an unsynchronized,
death defying rhythm.
Somebody's riffin'.

Over in the corner on the left side —
Some slide, others are tilting toward the action.
Getting packed like the main attraction.
Chairs scrape linoleum —
suddenly heard

because the din that we were lost in
is now gone.

A loud CRACK,
followed by two in quick succession.
A second suspension.
Silence ignites the tension…

Then it lets loose:
A brown hand spied holding the steel,
changing direction.
The crowd scatters to the lone exit.

The corners are packed.
A large speaker tumbles over.
One girl slides in a puddle when jumping over
a brown jacket
hunched over.
Now it's a loner.
The brown hand reveals its owner.

The chasm grows into an open tremor.
Wild eyes say "Get the FUCK out my way!"
We move collectively,
But not together, see?
'Cause it's survival's for the fittest.
Stray bullets in easy targets.
Sure death for any witness.

Suddenly cold,
The heat of two minutes before is dampened,
like the spreading darkness on the floor.
And some voice is screaming in pain —
somewhere in vain, for we hear and don't hear.
The competition for the exit is in full gear.

Who'll make it? Who'll live to see tomorrow?
Who'll be shaking?
Who will be a shell — hollow?

I reach the door, squeeze and shove —
a cold wind hits,
but fuck a jacket. I'm almost out —
but the crowd hits smack into a wall of blue.
Black irons control the movement backwards.

Hands fly upwards to meet the ceiling.
Eyes get wide. My heart skips.
Will MY statistics be in forensics when the lights hits?
Fear paralyzes.

"Nobody move!" "Get the FUCK back!"
I'm grabbed,
slapped smack into the bar near the front.
I can almost feel the bullets pummeling into my skull.
I'm pulled up, pushed and held in the position with the others.
Colorless lips bark the orders.

I can feel my heart caught in my stomach as an army
of blue clad enforcers
rush to the back
where the floor holds the borders for a
one
time
attack.
Shots riddle
off beat,
no syncopation.
Poppin' is deafening. Bullets are leveling
the brown hand to meet the
dark
drenched
floor.

Dark stains continue to pour.
3 bodies hold the spot where we dance no more.

One sob escapes a throat
held at bay beneath the booth.
More blue invade the dim lighted tomb
that holds the proof.
A triple hit/murder/suicide, one and the same.
Caught on the inside,
nobody wants to give their name.

The crime scene comes alive
with squads of plain clothes and uniforms
getting busy on us who got much to hide.

By time I hit the outside — it's dawn.
The sun hasn't shown its form,
but pink light illuminates the storm
that rages on the inside.
My pride took a fall.
I feel like my people,
we ain't got nothing at all.

My throat's bustin with a lump.
My nose quivers as I shiver.
The cold won't let me forget
that I went to be delivered
for just a moment in time
by beats and food for the brain.
The midnite was *al*right.
Now the dawn brings back the pain.

TaLe OF 2 CITIeS

featuring Manchilde of Butta Babees

Motion:

It's about a five hour drive to hear Mont Real get live
The soul controlla connect the whola the crowd like Motorola
There's no need for cellular so I can call that ass to task
You can't last inna the game with this tri-city duo
From the second I took the pen it's like I received the call
Now I got stacks and sacks of papers
My knap is full of killer verses
The virus infecting the central nervous
I'm systematic though I'm apt to tear it up with no rehearses
If you're dead-stock I got the hearses in fleets to complete it
The last lap to final resting place
you're gonna need it
Cause the tag team's been brewing
like a pot of mom's stew and
the rap audience is hungry
so I'm here to supply the nutrient
Good for the body
The mental's energized
by the ebbs and flow and the rise of Manchilde
Mo' the better

Bout time we set it straight to the letter
cause I intend to be here forever...

Manchilde:

When I was young I couldn't wait
Now my career is taking shape
You use to work at H MV when I passed you my demo tape
No record deal but I feel
That we still keeping it real
Travel way down on Greyhound
To push your sound in Mont Real
Now life's like snakes and ladders
It's like chess or Chinese checkers
I disowned my student loan
to press another batch of records
Hope this next release
will be a favorite amongst collectors
Hope the shoplifters won't get the CD past metal detectors
Friends — how many have em?
See how phone life can be?
Remember when you ripped the shit with Phat Al, Tony & me?
Remember when you played my tape on CIUT
Remember freestylin together down at 90.3?
I mean we good for the body
just like we was fresh fruit
Forget the sample cause Motion composed the whole organ loop
Now this lyrical ladee's chillin with the butta babees
And we're thrillin your life like Michael Jackson from the '80s

Dangerous

Chicago Winter '96... feat. Creole of Nu Bearth

Creole:

> I do it my way
> like Frank Sinatra
> Now I gotcha
> My mantras extort more heat than Iran Contra
> Guerillas —
> Paramilitary by any means necessary
> I'm scary
> like Ol' Dirty Bastard to Mariah Carey
> *I like it raw*
> Police don't shoot cars, they shoot niggas
> Like Cornbread running in the rain with his soda pop
> I couldn't break like Turbo but disco like an inferno
> Blowing over MCs who be like Annie singing *"Tomorrow"*
> I get illy puffing off them phillies
> in the chilly windy city
> Getting sychrolated to the midi
> *Can you hear me?*
> Let's break it down to the nitty gritty
> Like Lenny,
> Cause when it comes to phat rhymes I got plenty

Find yourself. Who you wanna be?
A real MC ain't the next MC
Look into my eyes and tell me what you see?
Eye and I's dilated from the THC
Mari-mama —
Eating whole crews like Jeffrey Dalmer
Flip and regurgitate your style while drinking water
I'm heavy
and some of y'all ain't ready for my lingo
Bingo
My afternoons be dog like Al Pacino's
They'll be no telivisualation of the revolution
We douching the whole Chi-Town sound of wack producing
Now who wanna say we grabbed they ass at the clip
You dusted and disgusted like E-40 and the Click
Pit row lay up style
Got the crowd like a Bull's game
Make me wanna take of my load and give it away
Hey, I'm dynamite like JJ
while you a chicken like Wilona
And I got more hustler than four corners
Squared, down to the root
yo, this is how we do
Representing one time
Allergics Crew
(a-choo!)

Motion:

Dangerously sane
My name synonymous with pain
Motion moves into your mind
and *Blaaow!*
Your train of thought's on the next course
If you're not prepared
you gettin' lost
But found, I'm staying grounded
Going under and over the mountain
I'm hounding
enemies who say I'm sick
Delinquent rebel-lion derelict
Some quick to convict
the Mother Mo — seriously mystical
Your material will pass
but not the residues of my blast
Blaaow! How'd you like it?
The lethal combo
Northside to Southside
Come to erect with the ammo-
nition — chemical explosion
Annihilation of the Shaytan
My ray is on
Infra black
Built to attack
then attach
My vibes onto your back
I clamp on then I'm latched

Can't shake me
Never play me
Because my game's predestiny
Rhyme-food the recipe
Now the best of me emanating
Oozing from your equipment
Even though with no technology
You'll still hear me in your mystic
mind - Meditate so you'll relate the A to Z
[*Motion times Creole manifest an MC*]
I'm on a mission through the music
More style than on a runway
So watch the model citizen
of the universal forte
I stray from the expected
I hit you when you're not looking
I'm causing tremors with decimals
Throw you off and your foundation's shooken
Us Blacks Are Deep
Deeper than Shamballah
In the middle of the earth
Nu Bearth will make your brain holler
"*Be born again!*"
Tho' it means that you'll be on the Blacklist
Fighting in a world of sex, money, greed and wackness
I back this vision
with a crew that knows no boundaries
You're looking in the sky for a god
and yo, you still ain't even found we

Resurrected in the T. Dot
Appearing in the Chi —
Nu Bearth of Nu Black
Representin' the *I to I*...

LOSING MY RELIGION

I think I'm losing my religion
like that track back in the day
Couldn't tell the last time you even closed your eyes to pray
The higher power confined to a once a week treat
To hear a preacher preach about the shit
that you've been doing all week
Your pops, he didn't go
Tho' moms, she's on point
Every Sunday dressed you up
So you could rock the whole joint
Plats in your hair
Sunday underwear
homemade dresses
Moving for a beating
if you'd get in any messes
Got infected by the ritual
Live wires in the front pews
Preacher making old ladies wet bringing the good news
Testify from the front lines
Mrs. Jones was always witnessing
About the souls she saved from all the

sins they've been committing
In her spare time
Since Mr. Jones done crossed the line
Caught in the park with a boy about nine
Now he's in jail
but never mind
Requesting prayers that the shadow hour will pass
Keep Sister Walker from walking in always
shaking that ass
Enticing young boys with shaky voices
and nervous hands
To be committing dark deeds with that
snake in they pants

Brother Junior's crying
cause his moms died
'Fore he was baptized
They say when they closed the coffin
She still had tears in her eyes
Now he's paying in the nite
when she appears
A white bible in her hand
Satan by her side
Bid him come
And now he's sprung
Got washed in the blood
Certified to eat the body
Preacher say that's the only way
we'll ever join the party

But in the meantime
You just watch from the sideline
And pray you got a little more time...

THE LOTTERY
for the brothers at the barbershop

If I won the lottery
the lottery, *yo*
I'd take the how-many million and put some money in the
    community
I'd buy a factory to manufacture wax
And if you're holding the ax, you get machete in your back
I'd buy a space and make myself a center
For ball, art and jams that we'd never fear to enter
I'd buy myself an island
In the Caribbean
Run all the tourist
Into the friggin' sea and
Purchase mad studio equipment
Continue on my mission for musical upliftment
I'd play the fool
Buy mad clothes
But invest in a home
cause niggas gotta own
Institute a school
To educate the youth
And build their self esteem with pure and simple truth

So *yo*, gimme the money
Oh shit, I need my ticket
Here's my loonie,
Pick me up a Quick Pick
'Cause Jack, I got your number
The combination boggles me
But it'll be a black day when I win the lottery.

Freestyle

Check the cris' chick
Handlin' your stiff clip
Watch her mangle it
Grabbing them jewels when you dangle it
Tight — I gotta strangle it
But bwoy, you couldn't hangle it
Lay back and watch how the acrobatic angle it
Me bruk him —
Gimme dat —
Who got the gritty dat
Make a nigga purr
Like he was a kitty kat?
Mo's the chick
Brown and smooth like milk chocolate
Put my face on your mix tape
If you wanna market it
I'm done wid dese pickney
Lacking in maturity
Don't wanna commit
But still yearn for my security
B, I think you're tripping
like a va-ca to J. A.

Me nah maylay

Other niggas got dynamite like they was J.J.

See, mi dey pon a nex flex

Spit spontaneous like turrets

Nigga acting nervous

When this chick set to service

Couldn't catch it

Stepped out the line and dropped your racket

The match went to Motion

Won the check and went to cash it

Me deyah like forever

Turn a man into a duppy

Some say my mouth's too clean

But noh know say my mind's dutty

So lemme d'weet

So me can eat and fill my belly

Have niggas on they knees

going down like they was Nelly

Me kill a ginnal

faster than light speeds in Orion

I body build with M Cs

Crunch on mics to get my iron

Sorta gravalishus

When I see a battle coming

Send niggas running like stockings

Leaving their bunions burning

Me nah inna eet

See a John Crow getting take out

Tried to come up in my cypher

But poor bwoy
Him couldn't make out.

LIVING IT...

It's funny sometimes
how beats, words and rhymes
fly out my mind
before I have a chance to catch it.
I try to find bits and pieces to fit —
find frame within the corridors of concrete —
defeating the purpose of what they're really there for.
These arrive at my landscape like a moving shot —
wide angle lens taking in
my urban scenes.
Close up —
I'm locked —
rooted in the spot
where I stop.
The beat drops.
Feet start to meet
tar black streets
keeping time in 4/4.
Score starts to roll —
people and bodies and
faces stroll,

voices and cars and conversations
fly past —
their blurred energies
enveloping me —
telling to me the tales
of other young cats
and females
feeling that
fa - fump
fa - fump
fa - fump
of the T.O.C's Mega-city breeze.
Winds of change hurricane my fate.
Fingers grab pens and add lines to a slate.
Connecting the dots, and creating works of art —
sparking the intellect
so our thoughts reflect
reality and fantasy
of life's living trek —
Murals on walls
and tapes up in your deck.
Pictures and poems and prose
and videos —
The way we move and walk and talk
— our clothes
Cornrows in Black hair.
Eyes on the prize
'cause they've never been there —
So we dream —

daring to swim upstream and
reveal a new day
in the rhymes we write
the walls we spray.
The goat-skins beating as we pray
Praising for the stages of life so we may
build for the next generation and lay
a foundation for a future,
finding a way
to keep hope in the youth.
Remember outta the mouths of babes —
the Truth.

We gotta show and prove in this time.
Invest in the next set to climb.
Hear the visions and pains in the lines
Taste the phrase we spray
Feel the wheel and come again of the DJ —
See the voices rise...
We arrive
pencils in hand
eyes to the skies
words on tongues and
dance moves in thighs —
and roles
ready to take to a stage
and control your moods and vibes
for a minute...
and share souls

The waves and tides of the city
the ebbs and flows.
Here on the millennial shore
                    there's more…

Put your hand to your heart.
Feel the very first drum beat
impart, disclose and convey —
telling our stories as old as the universe
and as young as our
very first day…
We live in knowing these internal gifts
Build our skills to
uprise
tear down
uplift.
Capture our time through
screen and script —
movie reels rewind
and we're onto the next
masterpiece.

This is a song for the living —
the living art.
This is a song for the young who
talent so
effortlessly.
This is a message for those who
hone,

promote

expose.

This is an ode for the beats,

and poems

and the prose.

This is a portrait of the city streets

that frame our visions

within the concrete

found between the corridors.

This is for the eternal lights that flame —

This is for the skies

    to which

        we soar.

STreeT SIGNS

I just reached my sixteenth year
A decade and a half alive
and now I wanna drive
The time is finally arrived
I put my head to the book
to get my 365
I strive to be admitted in a sense
But my license is a permit to be dense
Cause as I big up my chest
and feel proud of it
Another document in my hand don't mean shit
The curfew is set — Sign say "don't park."
Ain't no niggas allowed to lark after dark
from six to six,
In spring eight to eight
It's an unspoken law in a police state
Getting late
Must remember don't trespass
And get set for my next driving school class
So it's back to the grind
working over time

The more I grow
I learn the meaning of street signs.

Count about a thousand rules to learn
Points to lose and earn
Wait in line for your turn
But still we say "someday"
Can only go one way
Follow the arrows
You may not *or* you may move on
Don't stop to ask for help
Yield to everybody else but yourself
To keep your health you must drive real slowly
The beast man will hold me
and act like he know me
Punch my name in a computer
Laughing in the cruiser
Debating *should we shoot her?*
It's news to me
But there's a warning of danger
In the corner a laser being aimed by a stranger
Arranged in a line to proceed behind a leader
Freed in the graduating class when he passed
Got me on a traffic violation
Earned his citation
And the problem is mine?
It's just the meaning of street signs.

Let's take the highway
I know the law is the law
but I gotta do it my way
Go on and stay in your own lane
But I'm unceasing and unleashing like a railway train
So put up your barrier
I obstruct with a truck
Drive a dynamite carrier
A slow moving vehicle's about to get crushed
Put my soul to the pedal
I leave you in the dust
Stop?
I don't think so
I refuse to comply as I work out the kinks so
I can increase my traction
X marks the cross-walk
Mess up they flow of action
I write my own destination signs
Mark the route that I intend to find
Going a mile a minute
The race
I'm in it
Straight thru the finish on my
Own speed limit
The red
Warn that you're supposed to cease
The green
The power, motion, soul's released
The yellow

Movement proceed with caution
The black
The base that were proceeding on and
Tuff not tender
Can't surrender
In the race we a de top contenda
Tried and proven
The pace is moving
And in my mind
I've learned the meaning of street signs.

STREET VIBES

Walking down the block
I feel like I'm on auction
Living and existing in a dream of schemes
So I proceed with caution
They never understood about the neighbourhood
Tryna analyze — social-scientific lies
But every now and then I take a look around
Tune in to the sounds of stereos that's fading in the distance
Since I'm a witness with a bird's eye view
I gotta flock with the masses and get judged by few
Cause M.O.N.E.Y. rules everything
But beats and breaks remain on the outskirts of his take
They never could control the flow of soul that
sets and rises on the city with consistency
Yeah we're persistent
Surviving in a foreign land
We live in jams
entice the crowd to raise their hands
Look for God in the blackness of wax
Feet move on the concrete
Bricks buss my back

So I ask
Is the street for humanity
Or the does the struggle validate my own sanity
In order to cope I just *keep hope alive*
Make sense of the resonance and echo with the
Street vibe.

I-Land

give me the sun so my skin'll get browner
pass me the pen so I can make my first rhyme of the morning
my consciousness dawns with the season
the itching in my fingers tell me that I've got a reason
to take a trip to the nearest bus station
get my body moving cause my mind's revelating
that's called a motion, like the ocean
I'm moving congregations of the bowers
while the Hip Hop sways
so take it to the limit as we fly
you gots to get high
cause you never know when you're gonna go
life's a bitch
the rich get rich while the poor get none
I gotta reach to the island sun
I sing *Day-O*
cause me wan go home
but I don't have to roam if I can use my dome
emancipation on the nation of the islands
my land, *seen*
I gonna take it to the Caribbean...

Sad to say
I'm on my way
and I won't be gone for many a day
I feel my heart is down
I'm running around
Gotta reach to the place
where the peeps are brown...

the Black faces
shining with the traces
of Mother's contribution to the nu black races
the ancients have multiplied
peopled the earth
I'm here to make you aware that you're on my turf
I get real sick and tired of the fraud-out folks
and if I had a bit a cash I'd ship them out in boats
back to the lands of the ice and snow
while I bite into the skin of a sweet mango
the sandy beaches,
breezes through the trees bring me peace
with the natural mystic blowing through the air
and I release
it's a *positive vibration-yeah!*
irie ites
cause my mind is on the night
warm winds bring the ease from the pain and strife
I'm at one with my surroundings
bring me back to life

strive, rise and seek in the deep blue skies
as I move and view the world with the true black eyes...

I'm

Glad to say

I'm on my way

tho' I won't be gone for many a day

I feel my heart is down

I'm running around

Gotta reach to the place

where the peeps are brown...

For Ja(H)son

Antigua, Sept. 96

For many years, I've seen
this
*Un*known home — distant
yet near me
unattached yet still
clinging on
So often I dream of retreat
say *"so long"* to mean cold
streets of my birth, to a place
where Mother Earth with
my Father's heavens
kiss and birth babies
of sun, moon
and stars.
Late nites of rest
contested only by the chirping
My eyes widen open
as the first rays call in the day
Ears heard distant/near
callings — that
rooster squalling me to

awake and arise
Today — here at "home"
I can glance in skies
forever shut away
from everybody else's everyday
Bold seas entrap me
for there is nowhere to fall
and only too few to call me
from my destiny.
How can I leave now?
to retreat now to a next
unknown place — where a next
un*homed* race dwells
I recall my enchanted dances
that retell a story
that fell.
Now I am locked more
than ever in my
almost forever
I cling to… what?
To have… where?
No one really knows.
For now I'll wonder and
ponder my fate in the
here-lasting and
question my mind state
Only few
the *un*earthed
can really relate

to my yearnings
no pain, *nooo* earnin' for
the children that pray nite and day...
for a calling
A roof.
A root
A soil to reward the toil.
Where — so ever I
clamber
and stammer my uncertainties
I hold high
a head stricken by dis-ease
but still mightily pleased with itself
that by a god's grace
it got lifted off the shelf
of indifference
and not knowing and
not caring where we're going
I throw myself into searches
beyond state, school
and churches
see I to I with eyes
try for that mountain
overflow my own fountain and thank
heaven for the chance to pray,
relay and dance to
this internal rhythm
that rests — restless
eternally

Feel my furnace —
it burns steadily for you —
Home —
to light
my way to you — Home —
to cry a tune that will
lead me — Home
understanding, not fully but
knowing that over some rainbow
somewhere,
we
will
land
Home — always
forever — I demand
you to be here —
forever — I'll stand if you make
yourself known to me
I'll stand on guard for Thee
if only
I can guarantee — one
day — you will find me.

I'll be waiting
My appetite unsatiating
Be with me in my
dream (reality)
So I may be real
in this here
eternity

panther

Back in the days before I was born
A worn people packed up their traveling shoes
Sang new songs, chanted new chants
of Power.
The streets became a big
black cauldron
Hot with Ebony faces,
and Fros
and Fists.
Made the blacklist with
Stokelys and
Hueys
and Freds.
African queens became
soldiers
like Nzinga —
Angelas, Assatas, Erickas and Elaines
And all the others who had no names
Human vessels for tomorrow
The cat came back
Leaping from the dark rain forests

into the wilderness of Amerikkka.
and the People said
I'll be free,
or I'll be dead.

BLACK & WHITE

Looked in the paper today —
saw black faces in black
veils — holding up black
and white pictures
of a black man
killed by
white cops with
black guns
in the black of night
as he stood in the white
halls of his Boogie Down
Bronx building — still.
"He fit the description of
a black rapist" — said the
white lawyers when the
blacks came.
He clutched a black
wallet as the bullets
rained —
his white brain on the
floor. Clear tears

poured like blood in
the after math of
disaster —
and this black man is
no more.
white hands snatched
breath from his
brown body — with gleaming red eyes —
they pried
judged and
sentenced.
and now we hear
black voices sing
and white voices cry
and black words on
white paper
tell the story.
black hands grip
the sides as
black eyes peer into the
picture.
red boils inside.
blue light covers and
hides
as titles tell the tales of peaceful
resistance.
black man on the
way to death — and
this is what's

left.
Soft words from those
told to hold it down
and keep the people
calm, calm, calm.
black one from the black
land here in the white
man's Ca-naan.
black woman cries no
more 'cause she is
angry. black child
fights harder because of
confusion — now
becoming clearer.
these are the times —
no longer — days of the past —
it's reality.
see, black hip hop bops from
coast to coast and urb
to suburb — but
who tells the news to
enlighten the few
that really business?
I mean we're one. Right?
 — in the name of hip hop. But
hip hop don't stop
20-somethings from raising
black steels to black
faces — don't stop

white eyes from spying
outta tinted windows -
don't keep
faces from screaming "FREEZE"
in a snowfall of bullets —
don't cease the storm from
coming, the storm from
coming, the storm from
bringing down your
black body to meet
dark, drenched
floors.

now — black tongues
say softly — "we won't
take this any more."
... *Yeah right.*

Read the paper today.
a black man in black and white held by
black hands raised above
black faces.
Black veils
shade the grimace.
Black words tell the story
of a black man killed
by white cops in
the white halls
of the Boogie Down Bronx

darkness.
black
frowns will bring it
down —
will bring this
down —
will bring this...

black 'sistus' sat with
them — in the seat of
judgement —
brown women acquitted
blue boys in America's
fine white walls.
now there's more debt to
pay —
and the devil
can't pay
at all.

Revelation

wait a second
my existence is tested
realms are manifested
chucking badness utmost respected
reflecting reality's roles
but fraud modes are getting deflected
lust, greed, lies is what's elected to oval offices
high time and high crime the road to bigger bosses
allied forces count their losses
while niggas lose track — no memorials
remembering the casualties — Black
it be too easy to snap
reaction is fatal
the source divorced from the cradle
a womb/man born in sin
preacher say mankind's unstable
put my cards on the table
confess to get eternal blessing
laying to rest and
the casualties are left in
a state of peace lay low to escape the
natural beast

that keeps ghetto dwellas in the streets
see, pain's released
when I snatch my last breath
but the life I left's the first step
in the eternal test.
Revelation
mental stimulation
revealed meditation
bringing more strain than pain

NO TITLE

my fate's manipulated by
situations, scenarios
missions aborted
just like unwanted embryos
d & c's executed by physicians
placing the people in precarious positions

medicinal armegeddon
death's equated by the latest
infusions administrated to the
poor, sick and degraded
many addicted to quick fixes promoted
psychological sorrows
sucking barrels that are loaded

brains spray to shower passers-bye
ain't seeing nothing
hollow eyes are bluffing
alive behind the stuffing
the physical falls to mystical
but the spiritual is ill prepared
for life outside this atmosphere

residential

Hard
gray
stone
buildings
brick
upon
bricks
corners
full of sticks
Stone steps
leading to the
bleeding
hollow
   — seedlings sprouting
in the
stale
cold
air
windows
shut from the freshness
keeping silent

little
voices
  — the hollow
bouncing off
walls
  gray —
death cloaked,
white arms in
 black cloth
choked
young breath
from new, blushed
breasts —
unknowing but
the pain
  unshowing
except the
cool tears
    flowing
    from unheard
tongues

Residentials
containing
generations
of those
who revealed vital
survival
tactics

to those who
enclosed
and
  concealed —
lost cries
heard —
forbidden
familiar
words —
comforting
hands —
at mercy
of missionary
madness
  dead
cold
evil
  blandness —
in the
name of
  God...

Hail Mary
Mother of
  Race —
protect
  the
little in
an

invisible
  place
laying
in the
  middle
of this divisible space —
    uprooted
like new
blades of
grass —
moans as
dark
earth
is relinquished
of her
children —
  snatched
from her grasp —
wrenched
from clenched
fists —
though hearts
can't part —
Gray
on gray
stone
in gray
eyes
gaze gray

darts
to souls as
old as
the dawn —
decadent
lust
self-hate
hold
young
arms
young ears
hear
hoarse
whispers in
the dark.

Hail Mary
turns stone
deaf
in the
night
black
veils
leave
no trails
while
emissions
on pink
lips

linger
till
the last
breath —
left
engraved
in brains
tightened
by fright
fear
foresight
heightened
by fine lines
defining
the wrongs,
the rites
of passages
to
next
stages
of
life.
Higher ground
emerging like a fresh ray of light —
New virgins amongst the
dirty
little secrets
kept hidden in invisible texts
living like

leeches on the tongue
laying silently
till
the death comes
Creating yet
another tale
to
pass
on

Regrets

Like a heavy hole in your chest
No rest —
Hard to catch that last breath
I guess
I've been possessed by mind stress
Unless
it's an illusion
a joke or a test
I confess
disparity is messing up my clarity
Some out for check
Some brothers asking "marry me?"
Some run, tryna be free
Some hol' a key
Some done lock down
in Kingstown O.N.T.
Some roll a G
Some be selling dey body
Some catch the V.
Or jus' dash wey dem belly
Some sole alla we
Mos' sailed cross the sea

Some boss the beast
Some toss the beef
Some loss they teeth
Some gotta pay
to be digging out the meat
Yuh nah see it?
Regrets
Like a stone in the chest
No rest
Tryna catch that last breath
It's a mess
Can get possessed by mind stress
Unless I missed the lesson...

HIDeaway

I need a place
to hideaway from my transgression
my skin is forbidden my origin is never
hidden
secret eyes open wide
information is supplied
and I'm in check
for suspect I get arrest
Tested by the beast I never rest at night
there's no peace
cause in the night I'm burning up in cold fright
and perspiration
my dreams got me shaking
my eyes meet sunrise
and I'm thinking about escaping
I never knew who was who
true friends just turned foe
and now I'm locked up
deeper in the hole
it's counteraction
who got my back? some

clicking on the phone lets me know
that this shit is friggin' tapped, man
What I committed
some try to say it's wicked
but getting down to business means some
madness with a fucken mission
I can feel it
somebody's watching me
the more time flies
the more time spies have not forgotten me
It's got to be electric telekinesis
In the streets the beast pushing me to blow this
shit to pieces
I never blink
look over my shoulder as I think
so in these sands of time
I won't sink.

Free

Life's risky
the second I'm stepping out the door
Moms's in her room
pacing across the floor
It's a war — the game
Who's ready to spark this
No gain —
Unless I put my money on the market
My resource is human
I work for mankind
Sometimes I feel I'm losing my mind
'Cause the more you maintain
Then the more you're insane
Got my mental on lock
with that invisible chain
I strain —
I can't take it
Can't fake it
Where's the money? Will I make it?
Do what I got to do is take it?
Who's world is this

Yo, it's mine it's mine
While I'm living on the fringes?
What is this?
Some bad bwoy business
a-rule up in the higher levels
Never seen, seldom heard
So what's the word?
I splurge my lyrical expenditures
and invest in the next set to flex
So get yours. I get mine
and shine my diamonds daily
Some say:
where there's a will there's a way
Although I'm really making barely enough
But I'll erupt
with the right stuff to bust
Blow up with da bomb
'cause times are serious.

I sing *Amazing Grace*
how sweet the sound
Saved a wretch that could have never been found
Heaven-bound
Caught up in a rapture
Now the hereafter is full of laughter
And I hafta do the math to
Enlighten the minds and souls that got the hunger
Makes me wonder —
Back in the days we were first

but now we're under
Struggling for a food and clothes
and a roof and home —
I'm in a mood
but I won't moan
I'll fight
with every gene of my being
What's the meaning?
the mobb living in the concrete
and now we fiending for the C.R.E.A.M.
No longer content
to get a piece of the pie
to pay the rent
I got lands in the sands of the West Indies
My special education build me nations
across the sea
I know they ain't pleased,
but *yo*
I'ma make it…
Want it so bad that I can taste it

I'm free, free, free
(yeah, I'm finally)
free, free, free

THE LESSON

What a lesson
when your best
friend gets
sent to the
pen on lockdown
for 24-7
Away from the
block
and all the shit you use
to do when
you were
young.

What a lesson
when a man
dies at the
hands of another,
your man from time
when you
were
growing up,
way back then.

What a lesson
when your
pops drops outta
site
as easy as you
saying "good nite"
to the Gods
they say.

Now what
a lesson
when you
can't answer
the
question
"when will
my turn
turn
up
and will I
be
ready?"

Dear Marky

You are a Beautiful Black Bird —
Big and large in your presence
Gentle in your stance
As you *loom* over the room
Your smile lit up the Sun
Your face holds a shine
that will last for always —
Your voice — bellowed —
Lyrics —
that voice,
Raspy —
just *al*most on key,
would bring a song
from the depths of your heart
You rhymed the blues
You sang the
Oakwood-Vaughn Rd. news.
All the same from coast to coast —
You knew —
Now you've passed through —
telling more of the same

with those *beautiful* lips —
and eyes that spoke wonders —
Man, that shine —
like a big
brown
black
diamond.

You're not gone.
'Cause if you're gone
how come I still hear your tones?
Still see you sitting in the stairway
leaning them long bones
against a wall,
the banister,
Everywhere.
Lounging in that barbershop chair?
Yeah Marky,
you're still here —
the print imbedded forever
until we meet again
my friend.
So... no so long,
since so long
don't sound like no song
that you *ever* sung.
Yes Black Bird —
you
beautiful, *beautiful* Sun

Now the *real* journey has
begun
One Love, Marky
you're moving
on...

LIFE sentence
of the mothers and the brothers

My blocks are mystic
Stars and Statistics
Ladies pushin babies
that could end up in body bags
Maybe 'cause of red and blue rags.
or kids in doo rags.
Maybe a beast who *think* you got a
piece up in your school bag.
Swears he never knew that
this kid was just an average.
youth
who never held a pound or steel in his life.
Maybe that chick who gotta a knife
she's tryna give him jacket
In a fix @ 16, the crazy child
she couldn't handle it
Or the wrong place and time
On the block with just a dime
Copper say *"just scan the line —*
Point your finger —
You can trade another nigga for your crime."

Boy, you *still* do the time,
Take a shank in the back
Waiting on the phone line

Wouldn't hear when granny talked about signs
Dreaming dreams
that's talking 'bout you losing teeth
and still you went to the jam
And since your boy's boy
owes somebody else a grand
You take a shot for your man's man
That's the end to your Moms' Grand Plan.
That started when she pushed you in the
baby pram
Now she's that last to zip the bag
before they put it in the coroner's van...
Blocks are mystic
Stars and Statistics
Mothers dreaming of destiny
Wishing that they could guarantee
A life without the
tragedy

Praying their kisses and hugs will be enough
To save their baby boys
from a life that's rough.

CYCLE OF LIFE
for Bucky

Sadness
I feel sadness all around
resounding through my heart like a hollow point bullet
It's tearing apart the very seams of my being
Though I never knew, I see that hearing is believing
I look and listen
Tryna overstand the plan
The last time I saw you all I remember were your hands
That big, broad chest
your arms open real wide
Calling me to come and
Wrap myself inside
But now, your beautiful voice will never sing again
And now, your beautiful smile will not be seen my friend
though I never knew you on the daily
You were around consistently
Long time member of the A.T.C.
All Toronto Crew was what you represented
It's not the first time
but did we know, was it hinted?
Is this just a game where there are no second chances

If wishes come true
Can I ask you if your plans did?
Niggas always dreaming
Unrealized life
When your breath caught short
And the blade slashed thrice
It is finished
In our terms
Still yearning for your presence
If life is the teacher, the harder the life, the harder the lesson
to be learned and comprehended
It's ended premature
Desensitized to surprise
I feel like nothing can even floor me anymore
I'm sore, trying to think positively
You're on the other side
maybe you can be a guide within me
Giving me precise insight
Vision, precision
Sharp-shooting to truth
I gotta make the right decisions
though it's hard sometimes
Living in the madness
I'll keep my eye on the prize
And try to see above the sadness

It's the Cycle of life
We gotta strive for the living though it's hard sometimes.
Live tomorrow today

Cause when you step over the line
There's now time to look behind.

Untouchable now lies this
Body with closed eyes
and chin sunken in
Your ears don't even hear the cries
The din is deafening when the sad songs are ended
There's no smiles in the chapel
full of the lives that you befriended
22 years
And your friends and foes know
That the Buck stops here
you'll never see your daughter grow
No more morning suns will shine on this
Brown turned gray face
The whole thing seems fake
So I reach out to cop a touch
Cause looks deceive
You're cold and hard
Your hands now make me believe
You lay surrounded by silk
the guest of honor at a party filled with sadness
And just a little guilt
Death got much company
But still you left by yourself
We always put shit on the shelf
Much too busy to help
The race is running, always

tryna make tracks
20-20 is my vision now that I'm looking back
Regrets
I'm wondering if you're slumbering
In the never-ending cycle of life
Do we come again
Maybe we'll meet if in God we trust
From the alpha to omega, dust to dust
The cycle of life

It's the Cycle of life
We gotta strive for the living though it's hard sometimes.
Live tomorrow today
Cause when you step over the line
There's now time to look behind.

Afterword:
I close my eyes and think of you
And I wonder where you are…
I worry that some day we'll meet
You're never far…
I saw them put you in the ground
Now you're gone
Sometime I feel like you're still here
The afterlife…

For Kwesro (R.I.P.)

Rohan
I remember you
Round face
Mad bright eyes
Gorgeous smile
And tongue that spit for days
Lyrical swiftness on these
unsuspecting heads

I remember you
Flowing like water thru packed crowds
Burning like fire from a hot stage
Laying a foundation for a
movement to come
I remember
Pondering your fate
Listening to hours upon hours of long play
Leaving us open when you lay that
phat laugh on top of rap tracks
Metaphors that squeezed visual imageries
from sick analogies that made us see

Feel the haunt of your conviction
to rock precise with diction
directed at future fan bases with
hands raising and
mouths opened in "oooooh"
Slapping foreheads when your
lyrics to flow
blazed like flashing lightas
Lighting up these dark jam spaces
Witnessing the emergence of T.O.'s
next set to flex
Heard on sonic radio shows and
opening acts
Name slashed on street flyers
and debated on tops of lungs,
impassioned, heated, screaming
"who these niggas think they be?"
But *you* knew
2 times rougher that rock
Tuffer than overnite dumplin left on
counter tops
Harder than life on Chalkfarm blocks

Destined to walk that walk that
MCs born to battle
are sworn to travel
Committed at birth
Initiated on basement stages and

captured on tape
left here on earth

You knew,
Kwesro
cause last time I looked you in the eye
You spit like tomorrow wasn't possible
and last seconds were grasped like
oxygen
Final Hip Hop breath

Kwesro,
it's hard to let go
since you left so
suddenly
Slipped away
like the old folks say,
in your slumber
Leaving us to ponder
'Cause we can't overstand
Sometimes it's hard to believe
in *grander plans*
Because we feel you in the speaker
and we see you on the small screen
and we watch you in the register,
your resonance on the board-lights
flash, forever captured and fixed
in the mix
You mastered

21 years —
the mission's completed
21 years
of a young-known T.O. legend
21 years of
urban street tales
telling of this show
and that...

Your laugh reminds me
Lyrics rewinding
But soft spoken moments remain
in deep rememory
Thank you for the energy
we'll meet again
brother,
partner,
MC, lover, friend
Hip Hop Survivor,
some mother's son

But for now,
as you always say
Me gone...

NEGUS

Black King
I and I
bring sweet *salaams*
from princely lips
that draw deeply on
chalice tips
And speak words of wisdom,
and freedom and new days
Away from the systematic
babylon ways.
Breathe as the far-away
visions of sun-darkened people
flow in each movement
and smile as language
takes over, and fills me with
a hope
for brightened and darkened
tomorrows.
Yes. Yesterdays
have led us on the brink of death — but
survival has remained
victorious.

So we live
and give new wisdoms
to the ones that believe
And rejoice that there
are actually others
who really can
conceive.
03/21/94

negus1971 — 2000 thankyou

RHYME ON MY MIND *Pt. 2*

My lifetime is my lifeline
I write rhyme to find piece of mind and sometimes unwind
My radio's a shrine
Daily livications going to those who go before their time
I light the EQ
Lay the offering on a turntable
or a circle of tape
then I wait for me to be blessed —
Release stress
I send this to you, Negus
I feel this energy
that's deeper that a part of me
larger than astronomy
The university was hurting me
Thought it couldn't work for me
but now I see it's just a piece of me
and what I need to be
That's brighter than a star that shines so easily
but fizzles and dies
life spans I'll defy
Now I know why

I was given this position
The sound to move the body
and the word to make me listen...

THIS IS MY 1ST TIME

Winds

with change

re-arrange my fate

A future unknown

deciphers my state

I fear my experience

those to come, those forgotten

forsaken by some

Accepted by new tomorrows

Can I bury

the dead and the dusty

My fury be smoldered

to make myself trust me?

and those I allow to share in my dreams

the mornings thereafter

the comforter seems

to have leaped from my conscience

to appear on my sheet

An evening completed

But past nights compete

memoirs unspoken

Shadows awoken
Souls remain broken, but won't claim defeat
Sweeten the blows with a kiss of the day
Away to the vultures who hunt and who prey
But in knowing of the lights
that remain past the door
Gives strength on to carry
the strains of the chore
So grow me a home
where my heart lays
Laughs, frees, finds
content, breathes, loves
Me, stays
. First time hands hold
close, and hopes
as the mask falls
To reveal
almost
all.

mmmmmm

Baby, baby,
Black/brown man
I want to be your woman
Not for an evening
but for an eternity of
raised chests
  arched backs
    moist thighs
Surrender as my
lay-low love
  flips and dips you
slips you into the abyss of my
  spirit
Can you hear it?
the high-pitched cries
that grow from moans that
  flow and rise from
  you to I?
Your eyes slip tears which
drop and sit
on my half-closed lids
trying to hide my desperate wish

That I could keep and lose you
   at the very same time
There's no turning back
      Now you are mine
   and I fear to give in to this sweet
Sweet sublime
you have tasted my honey
   and licked your lips in satisfaction
therefore, I cannot run
You've clung to my shoulders
and asked me to hold you
Therefore,
   I cannot roll away
Now your burdens are mine
as I feel your weight under me
your bronze mouth pulls away
the claims of the prey
and the trouble days
   if only for a moment
As I allow myself to be smothered
in love that is *free*
I struggle for breath as I'm
pulled to the depths of
   unreason, and feeling and
long-forgotten caresses
   You move me
I swallow as my insides contract
with that fleeting fear that sits at the tip of
my womb.

Come soon, baby
Black/brown man
as I rock you in my essence
   and soothe you with my ebony touches.
Let me fill your nites
with wood fire stone
   for my earth is your home
The shield of our mahogany skins
protect us from the day
as we come together
   our bodies pray
and praise with tired song
for we received this gift
   that lifts into heavens
of heart-felt delight
The darkness takes over,
   our browns drift to black
and we fade
 gently,
with the night.

Dear_____

I love you
Your burdens are mine
Your joys and sorrows too
Your hope gives me hope
Your anger is my fear
Your seed has brought me life
And empty wombs to bear
I've seen the importance of your role
The immensity of your search
The wideness of our sea
the strangeness of your path — but can I fulfil
this responsibility?
Always I want to live through you
by you
or with you near my side
Or within the recess of my memory
Your words protect me
and guide
But your face, imprinted in my soul
leaves me no escape
to live

and grow and carry on
in any separate place
Your reddened eyes make me shed tears
That you can rarely spill
I long for the days when laughter abated
Our constant climb uphill
When quiet walks, unspoken talks
brought smiles that set me free
yet trapped me at the very same time
Within your destiny.

THE DOOR

In a world of pain
some shut their doors —
To keep the beating
fists of hate
From further bleeding
out their sores
They shut their doors.
They shut their doors.
In a world of pain
some shut their doors.
Outside stands
the hurt — the rage.
Yet still a voice
creeps beneath the frame
beckoning,
oh beckoning.
Some shut their doors
some bolt their locks
in a world of pain
keep safety in.
Some shut the doors

never again
to go and stand
to peek and see.
Afraid that cool breeze
cross the jamb
will kill them
will kill them.
In a world of pain
some shut life out
— tho still alive — in silent death
some shut the door
to block the view
of passersby and
inquiring minds.
Some slam it shut
when unexpectedly
one runs to come,
unwelcomed guest —
like a gust of wind
swings open the doors
Sees all within.
Some slam it shut —
wait breathlessly to
see or hear
another knock —
some keep it shut,
no more callers
no need for locks.
Some shut the door

in a world of pain
to keep a friendly
stopper — in
from ever being
invited in.
Some shut the door
Some shut the door
and never open it again.

ROLLO

Rollo was a bad man,
Rollo was a thief
Rollo came to my house and stole a piece of beef
Took me to the bedroom,
Laid me on the sheets
and touched me in the places where he knew that I was weak
I was at that time of my life — feeling lonely
He looked me in the eyes, saying that I was the only
One that he wanted to do
tonite
Yeah, Rollo's smooth
And he move too right
Ooooh, just the thought of that cool exterior —
body superior, make my whole interior roll
He took control, giving me body reactions
sliced it, diced it
Worked on every fraction of my being
You get the meaning
Every point
Had me burning real slow
like a well-rolled joint

I mean tightly,
and damn it's been a real long time
I know he has line,
but, the bwoy's fine
Girl,
you always talking 'bout sorrow
Besides
I'll take two pills tomorrow
I know, I know
Might be a hard one to swallow
but tonite?
There's Rollo.

INVASION OF THE BOOTY SNATCHA

Tonite
he never knew that
the wetness, the
wetness between
   my thighs
lay there in
expectation of
 your hands
waiting for entry
of your being into
mine,
waiting, as my
heart quickened,
and the breath in his
ear really said
"yes" to your
   advances.
He never knew that
his breath on my skin
was heating the places
where you had

nuzzled, and
licked and touched
the same spots you
soothe when I
am sleeping.
So he lay over
  me and
tried to leave an
  imprint in
my neck, tried
to lap his way
  into my
    memory —
unaware that
between his
lips and
my skin stood
  you.
Your fingers
  slipped
between his and
  opened my
    legs,
your tips
    touched me
  lightly
bringing a
    sweet pleasure
thru my body —

He moved and you
pushed your
way into me —
he told me
    "relax" and
all your voices
sung to me
"oh, baby, what about
        me..."
So I thanked
him for his
    medium
responded to
    his kisses —
his too
    forced tongue —
greeting him
    with
gritted teeth —
    opened
my eyes so I'd
    remember —
that this is not
    you.
Shook my
head so I'd
    forget that
this is not
    you

and attempted
to get lost in
his advances —
  slightly
intoxicated by
brown skin and
  deep
manly
  scents —
tried to
  concentrate on
my senses — in
  the here and
now —
  tried to
contain
  but —
  you
kept
  touching
me —
rubbing up
behind me —
pulling me
  down —
wrapping me up
  inside your
triceps
feeling my

spot —
rolling with me
on his mattress —
   I stopped.
Couldn't take
your magic
seeping into
my ordinary,
   my mundane —
my Friday nite
   fixer — just
to get me
      by —
couldn't stand to
accept young
   man fantasies
over big bwoy
dreams.
Couldn't simply
   close my eyes
      or open
my eyes to
help me escape
the darkness that
   your light has
      put me in.
So I
   stopped.
Held his

hand in
my wetness —
willed my
hips to
cease
felt you
teasing me
with your
teeth on my
nipple and
nails along
my spine -
felt him
breathing on
me, carving
on me:
"Please… come on… come
one… come… but
why?"
But
how could I
explain to
him
your eerie
presence in
that room,
your eyes
burning into
my back,

watching me
enjoy but not
enjoy, ravish
but refuse
tempted by his
convenience,
present here
on a Friday nite,
 so hot
when you're
 away.
So I stopped
'cause you were
 scaring me -
and just like the day you
 discover a
god and your own
conscience, I
see I am
never alone.
Why *won't*
you leave me
alone
 so I can indulge in all this life's pleasures
Why are
you *here*, conjured up
 in my
 mack-time
why can't you

leave me the

  tempestuous fleeting sweetness

of my

   booty

calls

my sex-friends

my

fuck buddies

my

lovers — we

 don't need

you here —

   but with you

it feels so good —

… I think.

Tonite,

he thought I

was teasing,

 or nervous

or scared, but

what he didn't

know was

that we had

  been invaded,

and that

 life can never be

the same

  when

a man slips in

between me, between me
and my lover's
   skin.

So I left him,
   and that bed
   and that room
      and his house
so I could
   come home
and let you
      in...

scene

Bright
  airy
and
  nice
the yellow
  walls
hold
  caged men
and freed
  women
who cling
  as the
bell
  rings.

sweetness

Sweetness
You're my weakness
my strength, desire
— I need this
smooth touch
to loosen,
linger here
with me a little while,
tasting your smile,
your smell
your voice,
dark and
dusty in the night...
I sleep alright
but still disturbed
by this presence that leaves me
— lonely
wanting for more
You feel me?
like liquid capacity fulling
my large cup

flowing over —
under your spell
still remembering your... *mmm*
smell,
locked within my nostrils
— teasing me from "reality."
I don't want it.

Now, possibility?
That's what feeds me
Afraid to love you
more than you are able to.
Me too.
But aware of your
delicious finish
triumphant return to my
past lives
where I lived on mountains and
prophesized
Sharing my
wisdom with
young girls
about
their
lovers
to
be
How to be free — loved
unconditionally,

passionately.
Lusciously
Leaving behind all dark lies
they heard in
somebody else's nite.
Not mine.
You see,
I've learned to love,
lovely,
letting fingers touch me
in every curvature of my
body
I'm not afraid
You see, because
Queens were made to accommodate
Kingly treasures.
Goddesses born to caress
divine shells and cradle
young emotions in the
nestle of their
breasts.
Meant to find and
give rest.
Meant to bless
with sharp and
soft kisses —
Meant to rise
above diminishing
intrusions — shutting our

eyes to spies'
pupils — that
tell lies
Wanting to
know our
truth,
But they can't
They just
sit by the sideline
dreaming about being but
can't be
Can't eat this
Can't taste this nutrition —
can't benefit from your protein —
can't
sink in your melanin
It's impossible, see,
Only one receptacle for your seed...

So they wait.

But can't stop my time
Can't interpret my riddim,
Can't catch it
Can actually hear my sighs —
But can't understand it
— But you can.
Feel
it.

Flow
Down
and Enjoy
my
Mystic.
Emotionally
stimulated
by
your
Physics.
Chemically
Balanced
by
your
Entrance.
Opened
by your manly
essence.
Loving every minute
of your arrival —
Surviving your descent
into my
crescent.
Slit open
with hoping
for a
moment of
your magic
Elastic strings

twinge tight tunes and
twang
poontang
melodies.

Soft screams in
the night pierce
our darkness.

Left unsaid
words by the
bedside.

Lay high in
uncovered
majesty
Protected by
deep blue shields
of night skies
simultaneously
occupied by
suns, moons and stars.

My universe explodes and I'm
led back to creation.
Spontaneous combustion
leads to big bangs
and noise
Rocking like a fire

in the cradle
of a parched earth.
Leaving me scorched
so when your rain
comes
I drink.

for Adonis

March 11

I don't fuck.
I do sweet things to your
body that words cannot
describe.
I crawl into your existence —
creep into your dreams —
hold you while you sleep —
you awake to that pleasured
hardness,
that must be let go.
My lips shiver against you —
vibrations arise from the core —
you can feel it — pulsating like a
heart beat — till you can't
think — *just damn — ooh baby —*
I can't take it! Don't Stop.
You tell me — by that hand on
my head — running through my locks
running through my knots —
an *mmmm* slips from your throat —
now I can feel it — I swallow.
Can't let go now — fingers twitch —

backs writhe — I position
get ready for that sweet knead of
my flesh — like whole wheat dough —
in my heat — you rise — ready
steady — inside.
No time to wait —
though time stood still
three seconds ago —
my heart caught in my mind —
you ride —
you fly,
head backwards — breath to
the sky.
I grab on — take me with
you — I sighed — I'm coming
too.

OH

He took me by the hand
or rather by the feet
with his soft
white
fingers
teasing me from the sand where I stood —
whirlpool breeze turning into wind
his strong tidal
pulled at me
pushed me
but I wouldn't budge.
His hands slapped at my thighs
they jiggled
the sound of clapping against my skin
wanted to go
but I was scared
frightened of afraid of his
power to cover me
smother me in his
liquidity
suck my breath

as I gasp — swallowing
my death
Others would run to him
but not me...
I tiptoed — gently
slyly — feeling such
cautious movement
would make me less prone
to his chill —
first my toes — arches
ankles — calves —
My temperature rose and dipped
to meet his —
He played with my knees
licking them, turning me in
his pleasure — taking me
from behind
I lost my footing as he rushed to enter me
over my hips —
I could taste him on my lips
he rolled over —
breathing
as Nature turned on her axis —
carrying him over me
constantly — then pausing —
his previous force ebbs —
leaving me needing
wanting his touch
on me again...

where I had retreated
with unsure steps
now I edge forward
suddenly
I wanted him
to feel him on every part
my body left bare
no more was the tongue
lashing against my legs —
my stomach, my thighs
enough
No more could I stand to be teased from the
edge of the shore
beckoning me to come
silently he waits
made me stumble
deeper
making me
decide — dip into his wideness
deepness
longingness
to embrace with my feet firmly planted
spaced apart
ready to take him and not move away
ready to face him
my eyes to the sun
my face, lips heated
cooled moistened
licked the salt, tasted his juices — life giving

affirming as he
came — over and over
again
harder
and I stood
proud that I could take it
arms stretched to feel his massive weight around me
tearing at what I had left
I could feel his tears on my neck
the white fingers enveloping me
surrounding me
frothing at my back
the sun beat harder
brighter as she shined off his blueness
I breathed
I breathed and he became quiet again
now I could hear his voice whispering
rolling — loving
caressing
leading me back to shore
where I could lay
and rest.

Puerto Rico

J'ouvert

The night rumbles as the musky asphalt
drives into my
senses —
keeping
me awake.
I can't sleep — for
the night refuses
to rest —
and the sounds of thumping
boxes and sound systems
keep pounding thru my window —
keeping my eyes
wide and open.
The dusty air is
heavy
tonite — there's
anticipation —
as little souls
make merry amongst
the men.
Mothers
laughing with

mouths wide open.
Double-parked cars up and down the
block let you
know *tings a*
g'wan.
Tomorrow is
Carnival
and now time comes
to meet the sunrise
with reddened eyes.
Last days of summer
passed by like freight
trains — heavily,
noisily, swiftly —
soon out of sight.
Like the
rain — distant
music hangs in the
air with promise —
waiting — biding time,
Revving up for the
morning that
will catch some putting
on new lipstick, and
halter tops
some making fat baskets with
chicken and rice
some polishing parked cars
and lacing up

brand new

sneaks that will be blackened by the end of the day.

The pavement will

be pound tomorrow —

the stomping ground —

as worn feet beat

grapes into wine —

and our blood

runneth over —

Soulful sanctity in the

uproar of the

heat.

The riddims

bleeding like stolen

hearts — reminding —

reminding of the yesterdays

way

back

home.

Here in Babylon's concrete —

we meet

congregate on street

steps, with brown

stones where green

trees use to

greet.

A child runs in

the movement of the

night — unaware

that any of this was ever
going on.
A fog settles — illuminated
only by the ominous blue and white —
passing through
reigning silently those
whose excitement will not be
touched tonite.
Brothers walk on the
block —
more cars park,
side by side
bringing passengers to disappear like ghosts
thru
darkened doorways.
'Round stoops,
souls gather, and
gab and grasp —
holding on — and
releasing as
summer says it's last
goodbye.
But before you go,
Play On — one last dance
as we make like
a non existent
Tomorrow
as we dance, jump, sing
and the music

plays on —
Waving flags of
red, gold and green hues.
Come colored brightly to
offset the browns
the grays.
beat riddim into these streets
join the cracks with 2 steps,
back-back
into yesterday.
Raise yuh hand
and scream as the
heavens drown you
opening and parting
Eastern Parkway, like the
sea.
Keep wake, tonite
as those watching with the
mourning —
as we lay the
season to rest,
saying it's ode of
"Woi!..."
escape in the joy of merrymaking —
let our love
run down - let your
soul roll as thunderous
Praise
let your voice carry in

unified glory
the song of life
here — between the
bare-bones existence —
here amongst the
tight squeeze
here surrounded by the broken sidewalks
exploding at the seams —
as the distant rumble awakens and tears.
Keep on sister as the
earliest appears
and the boisterous laughter
still comes,
all the more forceful now,
for to relent is to
give in —
and the morning is fast approaching —
the wind easing her
closer —
there is no tomorrow —
for it is
now.

I might sleep tonite.
now knowing that I have
captured her in her essence
Walking in her element
blowing in her demeanor
beating on her dark

drum — I can
sleep now cause I have
released her — coming
I have met her — coming —
now I can rest to
make merry in
the blessing of the day...
and make peace with the morning.

brooklyn labour day's eve n.y.c.99

MOTION (Wendy Brathwaite) is a Hip Hop artist, radio show host, educator and poet. She formed her first Hip Hop crew "Nu Black Nation." The all-female crew compiled its first record and appeared on the album *The Gathering*, which received a Juno Award. Motion has been awarded "The Phenomenal Woman Award" for her contribution to Canadian music and the "Urban Music Award" for Best Radio in her tenth year as host of the *Masterplan Show* on CIUT 89.5 FM.

Motion has appeared on several albums, including *Motion: The Trilogy. Pt. 1*, *Rebel Alliance*, *Man In Motion*, *K.W.O.*, *Maestro's Breaking Hingez* and *Rap Essentials II*.